APPLE VISION PRO EFFECT

2024

The Essential user guide to living two lives and loving them both with the Vision Verse revolution and renaissance

Michael Morrison

OVERVIEW

Step into the Portal: Welcome to the Vision Verse

Have you ever dreamed of soaring through fantastical landscapes, defying gravity in impossible arenas, or conversing with historical figures as if they were standing right beside you? The Apple Vision Pro isn't just a headset; it's a portal to a boundless realm of possibilities, blurring the lines between reality and the digital landscape. In this book, we'll be your guide on this exhilarating journey, equipping you with the knowledge and tools to navigate the vibrant expanse known as the Vision Verse.

Forget clunky controllers and awkward button-mashing. The Vision Verse responds to your natural gestures and the subtle movements of your gaze, immersing you in worlds tailored to your every whim. Imagine wielding virtual paint brushes that dance across your canvas, scaling towering mountains with a flick of your wrist, or engaging in thrilling interstellar chases with mere whispers of your voice. The Vision Verse is your playground, your canvas, your stage — a universe where the only limit is your imagination.

But like any uncharted territory, the Vision Verse demands both awe and respect. This book is more than just a user manual; it's a comprehensive guide to exploring this new frontier with safety, responsibility, and boundless enthusiasm. We'll delve into the intricacies of your Vision Pro, teach you how to master its intuitive controls, and guide you through the essential principles of navigating the digital realm with grace and confidence.

Whether you're a seasoned gamer seeking immersive adventures, a creative soul yearning for a limitless canvas, or simply a curious explorer eager to peek beyond the veil of reality, the Vision Verse awaits. In these pages, you'll find the map, the compass, and the spark of inspiration to embark on your own unique odyssey. So, strap on your Vision Pro, adjust your gaze, and prepare to step into a world where anything is possible. Welcome to the future, welcome to the Vision Verse, and welcome to the adventure!

CHAPTER ONE

Overview of the device and its capabilities

Welcome to the incredible world of Apple Vision Pro, where the boundaries between physical and digital realms fade away. This cutting-edge mixed reality headset unlocks a new dimension of possibilities, blurring the lines between seeing, interacting, and creating. In this chapter, we'll take you on a guided tour of Vision Pro, introducing its revolutionary features and capabilities.

Unveiling a Gateway to Mixed Reality:

Spatial Computing: Immerse yourself in a world where digital objects seamlessly integrate with your physical surroundings. Vision Pro utilizes advanced sensors and software to create a breathtaking illusion of depth and spatial awareness, opening doors to groundbreaking experiences.

High-Fidelity Visualization: Witness unparalleled clarity and detail with Vision Pro's dual micro-OLED displays, boasting a combined resolution of 23 million pixels. Prepare to be captivated by vibrant colors, razor-sharp visuals, and a field of view that expands your perception of reality.

Eye-Tracking Precision: Experience a new level of intuitiveness with Vision Pro's advanced eye-tracking technology. Your gaze becomes your command, enabling natural interactions with virtual objects and environments, fostering a deeper connection with the digital world.

Spatial Audio Reimagined: Let sound transport you with Vision Pro's custom-designed audio system. Spatial audio technology creates a 3D soundscape that dynamically adapts to your head movements, bringing virtual environments to life with pinpoint accuracy and immersive realism.

Apple Silicon Powerhouse: Vision Pro harnesses the power of a custom-designed dual-chip system. The M2 chip handles general computing tasks with unmatched efficiency, while the R1 chip specifically processes the deluge of sensory data, ensuring seamless performance and responsiveness.

Beyond Specifications: A Glimpse into Possibilities:

Imagine working on 3D models as if they were tangible objects floating in your workspace. Envision collaborating with colleagues across continents, feeling their virtual presence as if they were standing right beside you. Picture yourself stepping into breathtaking virtual landscapes, exploring uncharted territories and engaging in fantastical adventures.

With Vision Pro, these are not just futuristic fantasies, but tangible realities waiting to be discovered. This chapter has merely scratched the surface of what Vision Pro offers. In the following chapters, we'll delve deeper into each of these remarkable features, equipping you with the knowledge and skills to unlock the full potential of this revolutionary device.

Get ready to embark on a journey that transcends the limitations of the physical world. Welcome to the dawn of mixed reality, welcome to Apple Vision Pro.

System requirements and compatibility

Before embarking on your Apple Vision Pro adventure, it's crucial to ensure your existing devices can seamlessly connect and unlock the full potential of this groundbreaking technology. Here's a comprehensive guide to system requirements and compatibility:

Device Compatibility:

Supported Devices: Currently, Apple Vision Pro pairs seamlessly with iPhones and Macs equipped with compatible processors and software versions. Here's a breakdown:

iPhones: iPhone 14 Pro Max and Pro, iPhone 13 Pro Max and Pro, iPhone 12 Pro Max and Pro with iOS 17.0 or later

Macs: MacBook Pro (M1 Pro, M1 Max, M2 Pro, M2 Max) with macOS Ventura 13.2 or later

Future Compatibility: Apple plans to expand Vision Pro compatibility to additional devices in the future, including iPads and Apple TVs. Stay tuned for further updates!

Minimum Hardware Specifications:

While Vision Pro's processing power handles the heavy lifting, your iPhone or Mac needs to meet certain minimum hardware requirements to ensure smooth performance and optimal connectivity:

Processing Power:

- iPhones: A15 Bionic chip or later
- Macs: M1 Pro chip or later

Memory:

- iPhones: 8GB RAM or higher
- Macs: 16GB RAM or higher

Storage:

- iPhones: 256GB storage or higher recommended
- Macs: 512GB storage or higher recommended

Software Compatibility:

iOS: Version 17.0 or later is required for your iPhone to connect and interact with Apple Vision Pro.

macOS: Version 13.2 or later is required for your Mac to connect and interact with Apple Vision Pro.

Apps: The new App Store within Vision Pro offers numerous spatial apps and experiences, specifically designed for the device. However, most existing iPad and iPhone apps are also compatible and can be launched within Vision Pro, though their UI might not be fully optimized for the spatial environment.

Additional Considerations:

Internet Connection: Wi-Fi 6 or later is highly recommended for seamless streaming and downloading content within Vision Pro.

Accessibility: Apple Vision Pro offers various accessibility features such as voice control, eye tracking calibration options, and adjustable magnification to cater to diverse needs.

Remember, these are the minimum requirements. For an optimal experience, exceeding these specifications is always recommended.

What's included in the box

As you eagerly await your Apple Vision Pro, anticipation builds. What treasures lie within that sleek packaging? Here's a rundown of what awaits you:

The Star of the Show:

Apple Vision Pro Headset: The centerpiece of your mixed reality journey, this lightweight yet sophisticated headset boasts advanced sensors, stunning displays, and intuitive controls.

Comfort and Customization:

Solo Knit Band and Dual Loop Band: Choose between the minimalist comfort of the Solo Knit band or the added stability of the Dual Loop band, ensuring a perfect fit for any head shape.

Light Seal and Light Seal Cushions: Immerse yourself fully in the virtual world with the light seal, blocking out ambient light. Two cushion sizes allow for further personalization.

Power and Connection:

Apple Vision Pro Cover: Protect your headset when not in use with this sleek and stylish cover.

Battery: Enjoy extended exploration of the spatial world with the included rechargeable battery.

USB-C Charge Cable and USB-C Power Adapter: Keep your Vision Pro powered up with these essential accessories.

A Touch of Apple Magic:

Polishing Cloth: Maintain the pristine appearance of your headset with this high-quality microfiber cloth.

Remember, this is not just a collection of objects; it's a gateway to a whole new dimension. Each item plays a crucial role in unlocking the full potential of Apple Vision Pro and ensuring a comfortable, immersive, and truly unforgettable experience.

Additional Notes:

- Some retailers might offer bundle options with additional accessories like hand controllers or VR game codes.
- Apple might offer optional purchase of extra Light Seal Cushions in different sizes for even more personalized comfort.

CHAPTER TWO

Setting Up Your Apple Vision Pro: Assembling the headset and controllers

Now that you've unveiled your Apple Vision Pro and marveled at its sleek design, it's time to embark on the thrilling adventure of setup! This chapter will guide you through the simple process of assembling your headset and controllers, preparing you for your first foray into mixed reality.

Ready, Set, Assemble!

1. Headset Preparation:

Attaching the Solo Knit Band or Dual Loop Band: Slide the chosen band into the slots on either side of the headset, ensuring a secure click. Experiment with both options to find your perfect fit for comfort and stability.

Light Seal and Cushion Installation: Choose your preferred cushion size (small or medium) and attach it snugly to the light seal. Insert the complete assembly into the front portion of the headset until you hear a satisfying click.

Power Button and Charging Port: Familiarize yourself with the power button on the rear of the right side and the USB-C charging port on the left side.

2. Unveiling the Hand Controllers:

Grip and Trigger Buttons: Grip each controller comfortably, noting the natural placement of your fingers on the trigger and action buttons. Explore the additional menu button and joystick on each controller.

Pairing the Controllers: Press and hold the power button on each controller simultaneously until they flash blue. On your iPhone or Mac, follow the on-screen instructions to complete the pairing process.

3. Calibration and Fine-Tuning:

Eye Tracking Calibration: Put on the headset and follow the on-screen prompts to calibrate your eye tracking, ensuring precise control and natural interactions within the virtual world.

Interpupillary Distance (IPD) Adjustment: Use the dedicated dial on the headset to adjust the distance between the lenses for optimal focus and visual comfort.

Congratulations! You've successfully assembled your Apple Vision Pro and taken the first steps towards unlocking a world of limitless possibilities. In the next chapter, we'll explore the intuitive world of visionOS, your gateway to navigating and interacting with the mixed reality landscape.

Additional Tips:

- Download the Apple Vision Pro companion app on your iPhone or Mac for additional setup options and tutorials.
- Keep the light seal and cushions clean and dry for optimal comfort and hygiene.
- Practice using the hand controller buttons and gestures in a familiar environment before venturing into VR experiences.

Charging the device

Keeping Your Vision Pro Powered: A Guide to Charging

Before you plunge headfirst into the mesmerizing world of mixed reality, ensure your Apple Vision Pro is fully charged and ready for anything. This chapter delves into the simple yet crucial details of keeping your headset at peak performance.

Understanding the Power Play:

Apple Vision Pro boasts a long-lasting battery, allowing you to explore the wonders of spatial computing for hours on end. However, eventually, even the most enduring adventurer needs a power boost. Here's what you need to know about recharging your headset:

1. Battery Life and Charging Time:

Depending on usage intensity, the Vision Pro battery can last up to 8 hours of continuous usage. This includes watching movies, playing games, or exploring AR environments.

Recharge time from fully depleted to 100% takes approximately 2 hours using the included USB-C cable and power adapter.

2. Charging Methods:

USB-C Port: The most convenient option, simply connect the included USB-C cable to the charging port on the left side of the headset and plug it into the provided power adapter.

Wireless Charging (Optional): Apple plans to release a wireless charging dock (sold separately) in the future, allowing you to conveniently replenish your Vision Pro's battery without cables.

3. Charging Tips:

For optimal battery life, avoid leaving the Vision Pro on standby for extended periods. Turn it off when not in use.

- While using the headset, adjust the brightness level based on ambient lighting to optimize battery consumption.
- Consider purchasing an additional USB-C cable or power adapter for convenient charging options on the go.

4. Battery Health and Replacement:

- Apple Vision Pro comes with a built-in battery health indicator, notifying you when the battery needs replacement.
- Authorized Apple service providers can handle battery replacements at a later date.

Remember, a fully charged Vision Pro is your passport to endless mixed reality adventures. By understanding the charging methods and adopting helpful tips, you can ensure your device is always ready to transport you to new worlds.

Bonus Tip:

Download the Apple Vision Pro companion app to monitor your battery level and receive charging notifications on your iPhone or Mac.

Connecting to your iPhone or Mac

With your headset assembled and powered up, it's time to forge the crucial connection between your Apple Vision Pro and the familiar world of your iPhone or Mac. This simple yet empowering bridge unlocks the gateway to a universe of possibilities in mixed reality.

Choosing Your Path:

Apple Vision Pro offers two connectivity options, each tailoring the experience to your preferences:

1. iPhone Companion:

Wireless Freedom: Enjoy the untethered joy of wireless connection via Bluetooth Low Energy (BLE).

Move freely within your space, immerse yourself in VR experiences, and interact with AR content, all without the constraints of cables.

Instant Accessibility: Seamlessly launch Vision Pro apps and experiences directly from your iPhone, making it your handy command center for navigating the mixed reality world.

Shared Content and Experiences: Share photos, videos, and even your iPhone screen within the Vision Pro environment, blurring the lines between physical and digital with your loved ones.

2. Mac Powerhouse:

Cinematic Immersion: Transform your Vision Pro into your personal VR cinema, connecting it directly to your

Mac via a USB-C cable. Experience unparalleled visual fidelity and sound quality with dedicated video and audio processing through your Mac.

Multitasking Mastery: Drag and drop files, launch desktop applications, and even use your Mac's keyboard and trackpad while within Vision Pro. This wired connection unleashes the full potential of mixed reality for productivity and creative workflows.

The Art of Connection:

Regardless of your chosen path, connecting your Vision Pro is a breeze:

iPhone: Ensure your iPhone is running iOS 17.0 or later and Bluetooth is enabled. On your iPhone, launch the Apple Vision Pro companion app and follow the on-screen instructions to pair your devices.

Mac: Ensure your Mac is running macOS Ventura 13.2 or later. Connect your Vision Pro to your Mac using the provided USB-C cable. Your Mac will automatically detect the headset and configure the connection.

Ready to Explore:

With the connection established, the mixed reality playground awaits. Whether you choose the convenient freedom of iPhone or the immersive power of Mac, your Vision Pro becomes an extension of your digital self, bridging the gap between physical and virtual realms.

Bonus Tip:

Experiment with both connection options to discover which setup best suits your preferences and activities. Enjoy the flexibility and seamless transition between iPhone and Mac connectivity for a truly versatile mixed reality experience.

Calibrating the headset and controllers

Your Apple Vision Pro is assembled, charged, and connected – now it's time to fine-tune the experience for perfect immersion and control. This chapter guides you through the simple yet crucial process of calibrating your headset and controllers, ensuring precise interactions and natural movements within the mixed reality world.

Step into Focus: Eye Tracking Calibration

Apple Vision Pro's cutting-edge eye tracking technology unlocks a new level of intuitive interaction. To ensure accuracy, follow these steps:

1. Put on the headset and relax in a well-lit environment.

2. Follow the on-screen prompts, focusing on specific points at varying distances. This helps the system map your eye movements with precise detail.

3. Repeat the process if prompted. Calibration accuracy is crucial for natural gaze-based control and optimal comfort.

Fine-Tuning for Comfort: Interpupillary Distance (IPD) Adjustment

The distance between your pupils (IPD) is unique to you, and ensuring a perfect match in the virtual world is key to visual comfort and focus. Here's how to adjust the IPD:

1. Look at a distant object in the real world.

2. Use the IPD adjustment dial on the side of the headset until the virtual image of the object appears sharp and single.Don't strain your eyes!

3. Repeat the process if needed. Finding the right IPD setting might take a few tries, so be patient and trust your eyes.

Mastering the Tools: Hand Controller Calibration

Your hand controllers are your keys to interacting with the virtual world. To ensure precise tracking and response:

1. Hold both controllers comfortably, pointing them forward.

2. Follow the on-screen prompts in the Vision Pro settings menu. You might be asked to move your hands in specific patterns or press buttons.

3. Repeat the process for each controller. Accurate calibration ensures smooth object manipulation, aiming in VR games, and natural gesture-based interactions.

Calibration: Your Passport to Precision

Taking the time to calibrate your Apple Vision Pro unlocks a world of seamless navigation and intuitive interactions. With accurate eye tracking, perfect IPD adjustment, and well-calibrated controllers, you'll move effortlessly through the mixed reality landscape, feeling your virtual actions mirror your real-world movements with exceptional precision.

Bonus Tip:

Regularly recalibrate your eye tracking and controllers, especially after extended use or if you experience any discomfort or tracking issues. A well-calibrated Vision Pro is a happy Vision Pro!

Customizing settings and preferences

Your Apple Vision Pro isn't just a device; it's an extension of you, a portal to a customized mixed reality universe. This chapter empowers you to tailor your experience to your unique preferences, ensuring comfort, convenience, and an experience that truly reflects your personal style.

Dive into Personalization:

Apple Vision Pro offers a plethora of settings and preferences to personalize your journey:

Visual Adjustments: Fine-tune brightness, contrast, and color temperature for optimal visual comfort and clarity, whether battling aliens in VR or sketching masterpieces in AR.

Audio Immersion: Experiment with spatial audio settings, adjusting the virtual soundstage to match your head movements and enhance the realism of your adventures.

Eye Tracking Tweaks: Choose how your gaze interacts with the world. Want to select objects instantly with a glance? Enable direct selection. Prefer a slower, focus-based approach? Opt for gaze dwell.

Gesture Control: Customize how you navigate and interact with your surroundings. Prefer the intuitiveness of hand gestures? Assign specific actions to swipes, pinches, and grabs. More of a button aficionado? Remap controller functions to match your muscle memory.

Accessibility Options: Apple Vision Pro caters to diverse needs. Adjust text size, enable voice control, and explore magnification settings to ensure everyone can comfortably explore the mixed reality landscape.

Beyond the Interface:

Personalization extends beyond the virtual realm:

Comfort is Key: Adjust the headband tension, replace the light seal cushions for a perfect fit, and explore comfort tips for extended use. A happy face makes for a happy explorer!

Home Sweet Home: Customize your Vision Pro home screen with your favorite apps and experiences, creating a familiar launchpad for your mixed reality escapades.

Sharing Your World: Capture screenshots and record videos of your adventures within Vision Pro, sharing them with friends and family to spread the magic of mixed reality.

Remember, this is your journey. Experiment, refine, and discover what settings and preferences make your Apple Vision Pro feel truly yours. The possibilities are endless!

Bonus Tip:

Explore pre-defined Vision Pro profiles like "Gamer," "Artist," or "Relaxation" for quick setup options tailored to specific activities.

CHAPTER THREE

Introducing visionOS

With your Apple Vision Pro primed and ready for action, it's time to step into the heart of the experience - visionOS. This intuitive and immersive operating system acts as your compass and command center, guiding you through the boundless possibilities of the mixed reality universe.

A Familiar Yet Futuristic Face:

At first glance, visionOS might feel oddly familiar. Its core elements - home screen, app menu, and notification center - resonate with the Apple ecosystem you know and love. But dive deeper, and you'll discover a layer of innovative magic woven into every interaction.

Navigating the New Frontier:

Let's embark on a tour of visionOS's key features:

Spatial Home Screen: Your Vision Pro home screen isn't a static grid of icons. It's a dynamic, spatial environment where your favorite apps and experiences float around you. Reach out with your hand or gaze to select and launch them, blurring the lines between physical and digital interaction.

Multitasking with Ease: Need to check a recipe while crafting a 3D model? visionOS lets you seamlessly open multiple apps in floating windows, multitasking across the physical and virtual worlds with intuitive ease.

Gestures are your Language: Forget clicking and scrolling. visionOS embraces natural hand gestures and eye tracking for effortless control. Point, grab, rotate, and navigate with the same intuitive movements you use in the real world.

Focus and Dwell: Want to select an object instantly with a quick glance? Enable "Focus." Prefer a slower, dwell-based approach for finer control? Opt for "Gaze." visionOS adapts to your preferred interaction style.

Voice Assistant at your Service: Siri becomes your ever-present guide in the mixed reality landscape. Ask questions, launch apps, and control elements hands-free, enhancing your exploration and ensuring smooth interactions.

Beyond the Basics:

visionOS offers a wealth of features for seasoned explorers:

App Library and App Store: Discover a curated selection of spatial apps and experiences specifically designed for Vision Pro, alongside familiar favourites optimized for the mixed reality environment.

SharePlay and Collaboration: Bring your friends and family into your virtual world. Watch movies together, collaborate on creative projects, or simply hang out in shared AR environments.

Notifications Reimagined: No more intrusive pop-ups. visionOS displays notifications subtly in your peripheral vision, ensuring you stay informed without breaking your immersion.

Accessibility for All: visionOS caters to diverse needs with voice control, adjustable text size, and magnification options, ensuring everyone can enjoy the magic of mixed reality.

This is just the tip of the iceberg. visionOS is a living, evolving platform constantly expanding its capabilities and features. As you delve deeper, you'll discover hidden gems, intuitive shortcuts, and personalized settings that make your Vision Pro experience truly your own.

Remember, visionOS is your gateway to boundless exploration. Embrace its intuitive charm, experiment with its innovative features, and let it guide you on an unforgettable journey into the future of computing.

Basic navigation and gestures

The physical world has its hands and feet, the digital world its clicks and scrolls. But in the mixed reality realm of visionOS, your movement becomes your language, your gestures, your commands. This chapter unveils the intuitive dance of navigation and gestures, empowering you to effortlessly glide through the boundless possibilities of your Apple Vision Pro.

Moving with Grace:

Imagine gliding gracefully through a virtual landscape, your hands a conductor's baton guiding your journey. In visionOS, navigation feels as natural as navigating your own living room:

Gaze and Dwell: Let your gaze be your compass. Focus on a point in the distance, and your virtual body gracefully glides towards it, the world shifting seamlessly around you. Hold your gaze longer for a slower, more immersive experience.

Point and Teleport: Need to cover vast distances in a blink? Extend your hand, pointing to your desired destination. A shimmering ring confirms your target, and a tap whisks you there in an instant. Teleport like a digital magician!

Walking in Place: Feeling nostalgic for familiar ground? Take a stroll in your real-world space, and your virtual avatar mirrors your movements, allowing you to explore digital worlds within the comfort of your own home.

The Language of Hands:

Beyond movement, your hands become powerful tools for interaction in visionOS. Here are some essential gestures:

Reach and Select: Extend your hand like a virtual conductor's baton and tap an object or app card to activate it. A simple gesture, a world of possibilities unleashed.

Pinch and Rotate: Want to examine a 3D model from all angles? Pinch your fingers together on the object and rotate it freely, feeling the virtual texture under your fingertips.

Swipe and Scroll: Familiar gestures take on new meaning. Swipe to navigate menus, scroll through lists, and even manipulate virtual objects with intuitive ease.

Thumbs Up and Down: Like or dislike, agree or disagree – these familiar gestures translate seamlessly to interacting with virtual content, offering quick and intuitive ways to express your preferences.

Mastering the Craft:

As you delve deeper into visionOS, your gestural vocabulary will expand:

Two-Finger Tap: This handy shortcut opens contextual menus, offering additional options for interacting with objects and environments.

Fist Clench: Need to escape a menu or close an app? Clench your fist – a powerful gesture for a quick retreat.

Air Grab: Objects in the virtual world become tangible with this gesture. Reach out and grab them, manipulate their size and position, and feel the digital weight in your virtual hands.

Remember, in visionOS, your body is your controller, your gestures your voice. Embrace the natural flow of navigation and hand interactions, and you'll unlock the full potential of your mixed reality journey. The vast cosmos of visionOS awaits your exploration, so step boldly forward and master the language of hands and movement!

Home screen and app menu

Your Apple Vision Pro's home screen isn't just a launchpad; it's a personalized canvas reflecting your unique mixed reality journey. This chapter dives into the heart of visionOS, guiding you through navigating, customizing, and mastering the home screen and app menu.

A Spatial Symphony:

Imagine a world where your favorite apps and experiences float around you, shimmering like stars in a digital galaxy. That's the magic of the visionOS home screen. Instead of static icons, you'll find interactive cards featuring vibrant visuals, enticing previews, and intuitive gestures waiting to be discovered.

Reaching for the Stars:

Interacting with your home screen is as natural as reaching out and touching the world around you:

Point and Select: Extend your hand like a virtual conductor, directing your gaze to the desired app card. A subtle blue ring confirms your focus, and a tap unleashes the experience.

Gaze and Dwell: Prefer a slower, more deliberate approach? Focus your gaze on an app card for a moment, and it gracefully floats closer, ready for launch.

Voice Command Maestro: Need something specific? Summon Siri with a simple "Hey Siri" and request app launches, information searches, or control adjustments hands-free.

Personalizing Your Universe:

Your home screen is a reflection of you. Here's how to make it shine:

Rearrange the Cosmos: Hold and drag app cards to customize their positions, creating constellations that reflect your priorities and preferences.

Hidden Gems: Swipe up on the home screen to access the app menu, a trove of curated spatial apps and familiar favorites optimized for the mixed reality world.

Quick Access Champions: Pin your most-used apps to the bottom edge of the home screen for instant launching, ensuring your favorite adventures are always a glance away.

Beyond the Essentials:

For seasoned explorers, the home screen offers hidden depths:

Hidden Folders: Group related apps into folders for a clutter-free, organized home screen. Double tap and hold a folder to access its contents with ease.

Spotlight Search: Can't remember the name of that fascinating AR art app? Swipe down on the home screen and activate Spotlight Search. Type a few keywords, and the perfect experience will emerge from the digital dust.

Dynamic Home Screens: Create custom home screens for different activities. Immerse yourself in a curated gaming arena or a tranquil meditation garden, instantly switching between personalized layouts with a single tap.

Remember, your home screen is more than just a starting point; it's a living testament to your mixed reality aspirations. So, personalize it, explore its depth, and let it become a springboard for countless adventures within the visionOS universe.**

CHAPTER FOUR

Using Augmented Reality (AR)

Placing apps and content in your physical environment

With your Apple Vision Pro's potent mix of reality and digital wizardry, it's time to step into the captivating realm of Augmented Reality (AR). This chapter equips you with the power to seamlessly blend virtual elements with your physical surroundings, transforming your everyday space into a canvas for creativity and exploration.

Imagine the possibilities:

Summon a virtual art gallery on your living room wall.

Learn to cook with holographic recipe projections floating above your kitchen counter.

Turn your backyard into a fantastical creature habitat for a thrilling AR adventure.

Placing the Magic:

Apple Vision Pro makes integrating AR experiences into your environment effortless:

Gaze and Place: Focus your gaze on a desired surface in your real world, like a wall or table. A shimmering blue ring confirms your selection. Tap the air, and the chosen AR app or content gracefully materializes before you.

Spatial Mapping: Your Vision Pro intelligently scans your surroundings, creating a digital map of your space. This allows AR elements to interact with and adapt to the real world, ensuring seamless integration and realistic shadows and lighting.

World Anchor: Want to keep your AR creations fixed in place? Use the World Anchor feature. This locks virtual elements to specific points in your physical environment, so they persist even if you move around.

Beyond Placement:

The magic of AR goes beyond simply placing content. Here's how to interact and personalize your AR experiences:

Pinch and Scale: Want a closer look at that virtual dinosaur in your backyard? Pinch your fingers together to zoom in, bringing the digital world closer to your physical realm.

Rotate and Move: Don't like the angle of that floating recipe projection? Simply reach out and rotate it with your hand, manipulating virtual objects as if they were real.

Multi-surface AR: Unleash the full potential of your space. Place AR elements on multiple surfaces around you, creating immersive and interactive environments that truly blur the lines between real and virtual.

Remember, this is just the beginning! Explore the ever-expanding library of AR apps and experiences designed specifically for Vision Pro. Discover hidden features, experiment with creative placement, and let your imagination run wild. Your physical world is now your AR canvas, ready to be painted with boundless possibilities.

Bonus Tip:

Use the "AR View" feature to preview how an AR app or experience will look in your surroundings before launching it. This lets you find the perfect placement and avoid surprises!

Interacting with virtual objects in the real world

With Apple Vision Pro's Augmented Reality (AR) magic, interacting with virtual objects in the real world becomes an immersive and intuitive experience. Here's how to unlock this exciting dimension:

Reach Out and Touch the Unseen:

Air Tap and Grab: Forget clunky controllers! Extend your hand and "air tap" a virtual object to select it. Feeling adventurous? "Air grab" and manipulate its size, position, and rotation as if it were physically present.

Hand Gestures: Unleash your inner conductor! Swipe, pinch, and rotate your hand to interact with virtual objects naturally. Open a virtual drawer with a swiping motion, scale a holographic model with a pinch, or adjust the lighting of a virtual lamp with a twist.

Voice Control: Feeling hands-free? Use Siri to interact with virtual objects. Say "open the virtual door" or "change the color of the flower" and watch your commands come to life in the real world.

Beyond Basic Interactions:

Physical Feedback: Feeling is believing! Apple Vision Pro utilizes subtle haptic feedback in your hand controller to simulate the texture and weight of virtual objects. This adds a layer of realism to your interactions, making them feel truly tangible.

Spatial Awareness: Your Vision Pro tracks your movements and surroundings, allowing virtual objects to react and adapt to your physical presence. Knock over a virtual vase in AR, and watch it shatter just like a real one (without the mess!).

Multi-user Collaboration: Share the AR experience! Multiple users with Vision Pro can interact with the same virtual objects in the same physical space, fostering collaboration and shared discovery. Build a virtual fort together, play AR games against each other, or design a virtual garden as a team.

Remember, your physical actions are your bridge to the virtual world. Explore different gestures, experiment with voice commands, and harness the power of spatial awareness to unlock the full potential of interacting with virtual objects in AR. Your Vision Pro awaits, ready to become your portal to a world where the boundaries between real and virtual melt away.

Bonus Tip:

Download AR apps specifically designed for hand interactions. These apps often feature puzzles, games, and creative activities that leverage the intuitive nature of touch and gesture, providing a delightful playground for exploring AR interactions.

Using ARKit for developers

Here's a guide to using ARKit for developers, incorporating safety guidelines:

Key Steps for Using ARKit:

1. Install Xcode: Ensure you have the latest version of Apple's development environment, Xcode, which includes ARKit development tools.

2. Create an ARKit Project: Use Xcode's templates to set up a new

project specifically designed for AR development.

3. Understand ARKit's Core Functionalities: Familiarize yourself with ARKit's key features:

- Scene Understanding: ARKit maps the real world, detecting planes, surfaces, and feature points.

- Tracking: It tracks the device's position and orientation in real-time, enabling virtual objects to stay anchored in the physical environment.

- Rendering: ARKit seamlessly blends virtual content with the real world, creating a realistic augmented reality experience.

4. Work with ARSCNView: This essential class is the primary view for

displaying AR content. It handles rendering, camera management, and scene interaction.

5. Add Virtual Objects: Use code to place virtual 3D objects, animations, and other content into the AR scene.

6. Interact with Virtual Objects: Implement user interactions like touch, gesture, and motion tracking to manipulate virtual objects and create engaging experiences.

7. Test Thoroughly: Conduct rigorous testing on various devices and in different environments to ensure a smooth and realistic AR experience.

Safety Considerations for ARKit Development:

- Privacy: Respect user privacy by obtaining clear consent before accessing sensitive information like camera or location data.

- Inclusive Design: Craft AR experiences that are accessible to users with diverse abilities and needs.

- Physical Safety: Avoid creating AR elements that could cause physical harm or disorient users in their real-world surroundings.

- Respectful Content: Design AR experiences that are mindful of cultural sensitivities and avoid promoting harmful stereotypes or biases.

- Ethical Considerations: Be mindful of the potential ethical implications of AR technology, such as its impact on social interactions, privacy, and data collection.

Additional Tips:

- Experiment with Apple's Sample Code: Explore Apple's ARKit sample code to learn best practices and discover creative possibilities.

- Stay Updated: Keep abreast of the latest ARKit features and advancements to incorporate them into your projects.

- Join the AR Developer Community: Connect with fellow AR developers to share knowledge, resources, and collaborate on innovative projects.

Remember, ARKit empowers you to create immersive and transformative experiences, but it's crucial to prioritize safety, ethics, and inclusivity throughout the development process.

CHAPTER FIVE

Exploring immersive virtual worlds

Your Apple Vision Pro isn't just a headset; it's a gateway to a universe of vibrant, immersive virtual worlds waiting to be explored. This chapter delves into the heart of the VR experience, offering tips and tricks to navigate, interact, and truly lose yourself in the boundless possibilities of digital realms.

Stepping into the Unknown:

Launching a VR app feels like taking a leap of faith. Don't worry, though! Here's how to make a smooth landing:

Calibrate for Comfort: Before embarking on your VR journey, ensure your Vision Pro is perfectly calibrated for your eyes and controllers. This maximizes visual comfort and ensures precise interactions.

Get Your Bearings: Upon entering a VR world, take a moment to familiarize yourself with your surroundings. Look around, identify key points of interest, and get a feel for the layout. Many VR experiences offer tutorial modes to ease you in.

Master the Locomotion: Moving around in VR can be daunting. Experiment with different locomotion options like teleportation, smooth movement, or even physical walking in place. Find what feels comfortable and natural for you.

Interacting with the Digital Cosmos:

Once acclimated, it's time to connect with the virtual world:

Reach Out and Touch: Don't hesitate to extend your hand and interact with objects. Point, grab, manipulate, and even build – VR environments often respond to your gestures in intuitive ways.

Voice is Your Ally: Remember Siri? She's your guide in VR too! Use voice commands to navigate menus, activate objects, or even ask for help if you get lost.

Embrace Your Inner Hero: Many VR experiences involve action and adventure. Dodge enemy attacks, solve puzzles, and even engage in epic battles – your movements become your actions, immersing you completely in the narrative.

Beyond the Basics:

Seasoned VR explorers can delve deeper:

Social Connections: Gather your friends and explore VR worlds together! Multiplayer experiences allow you to collaborate, compete, and build lasting memories in shared digital landscapes.

Customize Your Reality: Some VR experiences let you tinker with the environment, tailoring it to your preferences. Change the lighting, adjust the music, or even create your own virtual spaces to express your individuality.

Push the Boundaries: VR development is constantly evolving. Experiment with cutting-edge experiences that utilize haptic feedback, scent generators, and even omnidirectional treadmills to blur the lines between reality and the digital realm.

Remember, the key to exploring immersive virtual worlds is to dive in with an open mind and a sense of wonder. Experiment, embrace the unfamiliar, and let your imagination guide you. The infinite possibilities within your Apple Vision Pro await!**

Bonus Tip:

Check out VR platforms like App Store for recommendations and curated lists of immersive experiences tailored to your interests. From breathtaking nature documentaries to thrilling fantasy adventures, the world of VR offers something for everyone.

Playing VR games and experiences

Get ready to unleash your inner gamer and embark on unforgettable adventures as your Apple Vision Pro transports you to the heart of breathtaking VR games and experiences. This chapter equips you with the knowledge and tips to navigate this exciting realm, maximizing your enjoyment and conquering every challenge in style.

Gearing Up for Glory:

Before entering the virtual arena, ensure you're prepared:

Clear the Battlefield: Create a safe and obstacle-free play area in your real environment to allow for uninhibited movement.

Charge Up: Keep your Vision Pro well-charged to avoid mid-battle battery woes and maintain uninterrupted immersion.

Calibrate for Precision: Fine-tune your headset and controllers for optimal visual comfort and responsive interactions. Every pixel and button press counts!

Conquering the Controls:

Mastering movement and interaction is key to VR gaming success:

Move Like a Pro: Experiment with different locomotion options like teleportation, smooth movement, or even physical walking in place. Find what feels natural and allows you to navigate environments with ease.

Become a Gesture Guru: Reach out and interact with objects in the virtual world. Grab weapons, pull levers, and solve puzzles using intuitive hand gestures. Remember, your movements shape your reality!

Voice Commands are Your Secret Weapon: Don't underestimate the power of Siri! Use voice commands to activate items, switch weapons, or even call for backup - keeping your focus on the action.

Embracing the Genre:

The VR gaming landscape is vast and diverse, offering an experience for every type of gamer:

Action-Packed Adventures: Immerse yourself in thrilling stories where you're the hero. Dodge bullets, solve mysteries, and battle epic bosses in immersive first-person experiences.

Puzzling Pastimes: Put your mind to the test with VR puzzles that challenge your spatial reasoning and logic skills. Explore intricate environments, manipulate objects, and unravel secrets to emerge victorious.

Social Synergy: Gather your friends and squad up for epic multiplayer VR battles. Coordinate strategies, work together to achieve objectives, and create lasting memories in shared virtual arenas.

Relax and Unwind:Escape the real world with calming VR experiences. Explore tranquil landscapes, meditate in serene environments, or even engage in virtual fishing expeditions for a dose of digital serenity.

Beyond the Basics:

For seasoned VR veterans, there's more to discover:

Push the Limits: Challenge yourself with advanced difficulty levels and master the intricacies of each game. Become a legendary strategist, a puzzle-solving virtuoso, or an unstoppable VR combatant.

Customize Your Experience: Many VR games offer personalization options. Choose your avatar, customize your weapons, and tailor the environments to your liking. Make your VR journey truly your own!

Explore Creative Horizons: Unleash your inner artist with VR painting and sculpting experiences. Bring your imagination to life in 3D, creating stunning works of art in a truly immersive environment.

Remember, VR gaming is more than just playing a game - it's an immersive experience that lets you step into your wildest dreams. So, strap on your Vision Pro, explore the boundless possibilities, and let the games begin!**

Bonus Tip:

Check out online communities and forums dedicated to VR gaming. These offer valuable resources, discussions, and recommendations to help you find the perfect VR games and experiences to match your interests and skill level.

Using RealityKit for developers

Here's a guide to using RealityKit for developers, incorporating best practices and safety considerations:

Key Steps for Using RealityKit:

1. Install Xcode:Ensure you have the latest version of Xcode, which includes RealityKit development tools.

2. Create a RealityKit Project: Use Xcode's templates to start a new

project specifically for AR or VR development.

3. Understand RealityKit's Core Concepts:

    - Entities: Building blocks representing virtual objects and characters.

    - Components: Add functionality like physics, rendering, animation, and audio to entities.

    - Anchoring: Attach virtual content to real-world surfaces or track its position in space.

4. Work with ARView and VRView: These views display AR and VR content, respectively.

5. Load and Create Assets: Import 3D models, textures, animations, and audio files to create immersive experiences.

6. Add Behaviors and Physics: Use components to create realistic interactions, animations, and physics-based simulations.

7. Handle User Interactions: Implement touch gestures, hand tracking, and other input methods for user control.

8. Test Thoroughly: Conduct rigorous testing on various devices and under different conditions to ensure performance and safety.

Best Practices for RealityKit Development:

- Optimize Assets: Use lightweight and efficient 3D models and textures to maintain smooth performance.

- Leverage Asynchronous Operations: Avoid blocking the main thread with heavy tasks to ensure smooth rendering and responsiveness.

- Utilize Entity Component System: Take advantage of the flexibility and modularity of RealityKit's ECS architecture to manage complexity and create reusable components.

- Consider Performance and Battery Life: Optimize visual fidelity and interactions to balance immersiveness with device resources.

Safety Considerations:

- Physical Safety: Design experiences that avoid collisions with real-world objects and prevent disorientation or discomfort for users.

- Accessibility: Craft experiences inclusive for users with visual, auditory, or motor impairments.

- Privacy: Respect user privacy by obtaining clear consent for camera and sensor usage, and handle sensitive data responsibly.

- Content Guidelines: Adhere to Apple's App Store guidelines to ensure appropriate content for all ages.

Additional Tips:

- Explore Apple's Sample Code: Learn best practices from Apple's RealityKit sample projects.

- Stay Updated: Keep abreast of the latest RealityKit features and advancements.

- Join the Developer Community: Connect with fellow developers to share knowledge and collaborate.

Remember, RealityKit empowers you to create compelling AR and VR experiences, but prioritize safety, accessibility, and ethical guidelines throughout the development process.

CHAPTER SIX

Interacting with Your Apple Vision Pro:

Mastering the Language of Motion: Hand Gestures and Eye Tracking in Your Apple Vision Pro

Your Apple Vision Pro isn't just a high-tech visor; it's a window to a world where your movements and gaze become your voice, your hands the conduits to a universe of digital possibilities. This chapter delves into the magic of interacting with your Vision Pro, unlocking the secrets of hand gestures and eye tracking to navigate effortlessly and express yourself intuitively.

Reaching for the Stars: Unleashing the Power of Hand Gestures.

Imagine commanding virtual landscapes with the grace of a conductor, your hands shaping the digital world around you. With Vision Pro, this isn't a fantasy; it's reality. Here's how to master the language of hand gestures:

Point and Select: Extend your hand like a virtual conductor's baton and focus on your desired object or app. A subtle blue ring confirms your intent, and a tap unleashes the experience. Simplicity at its finest!

Reach and Grab: Feeling adventurous? Stretch out your hand and "air grab" a virtual object. Rotate, resize, and manipulate it as if it were real, feeling the subtle haptic feedback that simulates its weight and texture.

Swipe and Scroll: Familiar gestures take on new meaning. Swipe to navigate menus, scroll through lists, and even paint in VR apps, your hand movements seamlessly translated into digital actions.

Thumbs Up and Down: Like or dislike, agree or disagree – these familiar gestures translate effortlessly to interacting with virtual content, offering quick and intuitive ways to express your preferences.

Beyond the Basics: Advanced Hand Gestures for Power Users

For seasoned explorers, the hand gesture repertoire expands:

Two-Finger Tap: This handy shortcut opens contextual menus, offering additional options for interacting with objects and environments.

Fist Clench: Need to escape a menu or close an app? Clench your fist – a powerful gesture for a quick retreat.

Air Grab and Throw:Feeling playful? Grab a virtual object and fling it through the air, watching it react according to realistic physics.

Two-Finger Pinch: Want a closer look at that intricate model in VR? Pinch your fingers together to zoom in, bringing the digital world closer to your physical realm.

The Dance of Your Gaze: Eye Tracking Takes Center Stage

Your eyes speak volumes, even in the digital realm. Vision Pro's eye tracking technology unlocks a new layer of interaction:

Focus and Dwell: Lock your gaze on an object for a moment, and it gracefully floats closer, inviting exploration. This slower, more deliberate approach is ideal for precise selection and detailed examination.

Gaze and Scroll: Let your eyes guide you. Focus on different points on a menu or list, and the content scrolls smoothly beneath your gaze, keeping your hands free for other interactions.

Blink and Confirm: Tired of tapping buttons? With gaze confirmation, a simple blink activates your selection, offering an effortless and intuitive way to make choices.

Direct your Attention: In AR, your gaze becomes a spotlight. Focus on specific points in your real-world environment to direct virtual elements, highlighting areas of interest and guiding others' attention within the shared space.

Remember, hand gestures and eye tracking are your windows to the boundless possibilities of your Vision Pro. Embrace the natural flow of movement and gaze, experiment with advanced interactions, and discover a world where communication transcends spoken words and takes form in the dance of your body and eyes.

Bonus Tip:

Combine hand gestures and eye tracking for even more intuitive control. For example, point at an object with your hand and then focus your gaze to activate it, creating a seamless connection between your physical and digital actions.

Using natural hand gestures to navigate and interact

Ditch the Controllers, Embrace the Fingers: Navigating and Interacting with Natural Hand Gestures on Your Apple Vision Pro

Forget clunky buttons and awkward joysticks! Your Apple Vision Pro opens the door to a world where your own hands become the ultimate controllers, navigating and interacting with virtual landscapes and digital interfaces with an intuitive grace that feels as natural as breathing. Let's dive into the fascinating world of natural hand gestures and unlock the full potential of your Vision Pro:

Pointing Your Way to Adventure:

Imagine effortlessly gliding through virtual worlds, your outstretched hand a conductor's baton directing your journey. With Vision Pro's precise hand tracking, a simple point towards a distant point of interest is all it takes to smoothly teleport there. No more button mashing, just a natural gesture and you're soaring through vibrant digital landscapes.

Reach Out and Touch the Unreal:

Feel the urge to get hands-on? Extend your palm and "air grab" a virtual object. Rotate it, resize it, even toss it through the air – the haptic feedback technology simulates its textures and weight, blurring the lines between the real and the virtual. Want to examine a delicate butterfly fluttering in your AR garden? Pinch your fingers together to zoom in, bringing the digital creature closer to your curious gaze.

Swipe Like a Jedi Master:

Familiar gestures take on new, powerful meanings. Swipe your hand to navigate menus, scroll through information streams, and even paint in VR applications. Your hand movements translate seamlessly into digital actions, letting you manipulate the virtual world with the fluid ease of a seasoned magician.

Thumbs Up, You're a Master:

Expressing preferences becomes as natural as breathing. A simple thumbs up or down lets you instantly like or dislike, agree or disagree. This intuitive gesture system makes navigating websites, interacting with VR experiences, and expressing your opinions more convenient and fun than ever before.

Beyond the Basics: Unlocking Advanced Gestures:

For seasoned explorers, the hand gesture repertoire offers even more possibilities:

- Two-Finger Tap: This handy shortcut opens contextual menus, revealing hidden options and deeper levels of interaction with objects and environments.

- Fist Clench: Need a quick escape? Clench your fist to instantly close an app or exit a menu – a powerful gesture for regaining control and refocusing your digital journey.

- Air Grab and Throw: Feeling playful? Grab a virtual object and fling it through the air, watching it react with realistic physics. Throw a snowball at a virtual snowman or launch a rocket into the VR sky – the possibilities are endless!

Remember, your hands are your voice in the digital realm. Embrace the intuitive and expressive power of natural hand gestures, experiment with advanced interactions, and discover a world where the boundaries between you and the technology you use melt away. Your Apple Vision Pro awaits, ready to be explored with the graceful dance of your own hands.

Bonus Tip:

Combine hand gestures with your voice for even more powerful control. Ask Siri to open an app while pointing your hand towards it, or call for a virtual tool as you reach out to grab it. Let your voice and gestures work in harmony to navigate the digital world with effortless fluency.

Leveraging eye tracking for enhanced control and immersion

Move over, clumsy controllers and button-mashing! Your Apple Vision Pro unlocks a new realm of interaction with its cutting-edge eye tracking technology. Prepare to ditch the physical and embrace the power of your gaze, transforming the way you navigate, interact, and experience the digital world.

Gaze and Dwell: Your Eyes Become a Conductor's Baton

Imagine gently guiding your focus like a spotlight, and virtual elements gracefully shift to meet your gaze. This is the magic of dwell selection. Fix your eyes on an object, and it slowly floats closer, inviting exploration.

Want to activate it? A simple blink confirms your choice, making selection as effortless as looking.

Scroll with Your Eyes: Reading Reimagined

Forget swiping! Eye tracking lets you scroll through texts, websites, and menus simply by shifting your gaze. No more reaching for your hand controller—the content smoothly flows beneath your eyes, keeping you immersed and in control. This intuitive system is perfect for long reading sessions or exploring vast virtual libraries.

Direct Your Attention: A Spotlight for the Mind

In augmented reality, your gaze becomes a powerful tool for guiding attention. Focus on specific points in your real-world environment to highlight elements for others in the shared space. Imagine showcasing hidden details of a painting to your friends or directing attention to interesting points of view during a virtual tour.

Beyond the Basics: Mastering Advanced Gaze Interactions**

For seasoned explorers, eye tracking offers even deeper control:

Quick Glance Menus: Access contextual menus with a swift eye movement. Focus on a specific area for a brief moment, and relevant options instantly appear, ready for selection with a blink.

Subtle Nuances, Big Impact: Express emotions and preferences like never before. Dilate your pupils to showcase excitement in VR games, or narrow your gaze to convey focus during virtual meetings.

Gaze and Gesture Combo: Combine the power of your eyes and hands for ultimate control. Point at an object with your hand, then focus your gaze to activate it, creating a seamless connection between physical and digital actions.

Remember, your eyes are windows to your soul, and in virtual reality, they become windows to worlds of possibility. Embrace the intuitive power of eye tracking, experiment with advanced interactions, and discover a deeper level of immersion in the digital realm. Your Apple Vision Pro awaits, ready to be explored through the lens of your gaze.

Bonus Tip:

Train your eye tracking skills! Play specific games and apps designed to challenge and improve your gaze control. The more you practice, the smoother and more intuitive your interactions in the digital world will become.

Customizing gesture and eye tracking settings

Your Apple Vision Pro isn't just a high-tech headset; it's a portal to personalized digital experiences. Just like tweaking your smartphone settings, you can fine-tune how you interact with it through gestures and eye tracking. Let's delve into the customization options, empowering you to craft a reality tailored to your unique preferences.

Hand Gesture Harmony:

- Sensitivity: Feeling like your gestures are too twitchy or sluggish? Adjust the sensitivity slider to create a perfect balance between swift responses and accidental activations.

- Dominant Hand: Lefty or righty? Set your dominant hand for intuitive point-and-select interactions. You can even switch dominance on the fly!

- Custom Gestures: Feeling creative? Apple Vision Pro lets you program simple custom gestures for specific actions. Want to silence a virtual call with a "shushing" motion? Make it happen!

Eye Tracking Elegance:

- Calibration is Key: Ensure your eye tracking is precise with regular calibration. Imagine trying to paint with a wobbly brush; inaccurate gaze control can be equally frustrating.

- Gaze Dwell Time: Adjust how long you need to focus on an object to activate it. Prefer lightning-fast selections? Shorten the dwell time. Need a more deliberate approach? Lengthen it!

- Blink Sensitivity: Not everyone blinks at the same rate. Customize the blink sensitivity to avoid accidental activations or frustrating non-registrations.

Bonus Tweaks:

- Haptic Feedback Intensity: Do you prefer subtle vibrations or a firmer handshake from your virtual objects? Customize the haptic feedback intensity for a truly personalized experience.

- Voice Assistant Trigger: Choose how you want to summon Siri. A simple "Hey Siri" or a dedicated tap on your virtual wristband – the choice is yours!

- Accessibility Options: Apple Vision Pro caters to diverse needs. Explore text-to-speech options, alternative input methods, and adjustable font sizes for a comfortable and inclusive experience.

Remember, customization is your key to unlocking the full potential of your Apple Vision Pro. Experiment, tweak, and play until your gestures and eye tracking feel like an extension of yourself. Your perfect digital reality awaits!

Extra Tip:

Share your custom settings! Create profiles for different activities or preferences, like a "gaming mode" with fast gestures and minimal haptic feedback, or a "relaxation mode" with slow dwell times and calming auditory feedback.

CHAPTER SEVEN

Voice Control and Siri

Using voice commands to control your Apple Vision Pro

Your Apple Vision Pro isn't just a headset; it's a digital haven where your voice becomes your ultimate command tool. Forget clunky buttons and awkward gestures – with Voice Control and Siri, navigating, interacting, and expressing yourself in the virtual world is as simple as speaking your mind. Let's delve into the magic of voice commands and unlock the full potential of your vocal prowess:

Commanding the Digital Landscape:

Imagine effortlessly dictating text in VR applications, whispering "open that app" to seamlessly launch your favorite program, or even requesting a virtual tour guide with a simple "take me to the Colosseum." Voice Control on Apple Vision Pro makes these fantasies a reality.

Siri, Your Ever-Present Assistant:

Need a helping hand, even in the digital realm? Siri is always a "Hey Siri" away, ready to assist you with a multitude of tasks:

Navigating the Menus: Feeling lost in VR? Ask Siri to find specific locations, open settings, or even adjust the lighting in your virtual environment.

Information at Your Fingertips: Curious about the history of that towering virtual castle? Ask Siri – she'll readily access and share information from the real world within your AR experience.

Stay Connected: Never miss a beat. Use Siri to make calls, send messages, or even control your smart home devices – all without leaving your immersive digital journey.

Beyond the Basics: Mastering Advanced Voice Control:

For seasoned explorers, the voice command repertoire offers even more possibilities:

Custom Voice Shortcuts: Tired of saying long phrases? Create custom voice shortcuts for frequently used actions. "Launch VR game" or "Show me Mars" – the possibilities are endless!

Dictation with Precision: Dictate emails, notes, and even in-game messages with remarkable accuracy. Voice Control recognizes punctuation and even different languages, making it your ultimate digital scribe.

Hands-Free Multitasking: Juggle virtual activities with ease. Use voice commands to pause music while exploring in VR, answer calls while designing in 3D, or switch between augmented reality apps without ever lifting a finger.

Remember, your voice is your passport to a world of effortless interaction in the digital realm. Embrace the power of Voice Control and Siri, experiment with advanced commands, and discover the freedom of navigating, interacting, and expressing yourself with the simple magic of your spoken words. Your Apple Vision Pro awaits, ready to listen and obey!

Bonus Tip:

Train your voice recognition! Practice using a variety of accents, tones, and speaking speeds to improve the accuracy of your voice commands. The more you interact with your Vision Pro through voice, the smoother and more personalized your digital experiences will become.

Asking Siri questions and performing actions hands-free

Move over, clunky buttons and awkward gestures! Your Apple Vision Pro, along with the ever-helpful Siri, lets you conquer both the real and virtual worlds with the power of your voice. Forget reaching for controllers or tapping menus – ask questions, issue commands, and perform actions seamlessly, hands-free. Let's delve into the magic of Siri and unlock the full potential of your vocal prowess:

Whispering Wishes to Siri:

Imagine exploring a breathtaking VR landscape while casually asking Siri, "What's the name of that mountain peak?" or requesting, "Show me historical photos of this ancient temple." Your curiosity becomes your command, with Siri readily accessing and presenting information within your immersive experience.

Hands-Free Heroics:

Need a helping hand without leaving your digital journey? Siri is your on-call assistant:

Navigation Ninja: Feeling lost in a sprawling virtual city? Ask Siri to "Find the nearest market" or "Guide me to the central plaza" – she'll become your digital cartographer, directing you with precise voice cues.

Information Alchemist: Curious about the intricate details of that virtual artwork? Ask Siri, "Explain the symbolism in this painting" or "Tell me the artist's biography." She'll readily weave information from the real world into your augmented reality experience.

Stay Connected, Always: Keep the real world at your fingertips. Use Siri to "Call Mom" while conquering a VR game, "Send a message to my team" in the midst of designing a 3D model, or control your smart home devices – all without ever missing a beat in your digital adventure.

Beyond the Basics: Mastering Advanced Siri Skills:

For seasoned explorers, the Siri repertoire offers even more possibilities:

Custom Shortcuts, Voice Activated: Tired of lengthy phrases? Create custom voice shortcuts for frequently used actions. "Launch space exploration app" or "Show me the news headlines" – the possibilities are endless!

Dictation Decoded: Dictate emails, notes, and even in-game messages with remarkable accuracy. Siri recognizes punctuation and even different languages, making her your ultimate digital scribe.

Multitasking Maestro: Juggle virtual activities with ease. Use voice commands to "Pause music while exploring the jungle" or "Answer the call while building this robot" – switch between tasks and control your digital environment effortlessly.

Remember, your voice is your passport to a world of effortless interaction in both the real and virtual realms.

Embrace the power of Siri, experiment with advanced skills, and discover the freedom of navigating, interacting, and expressing yourself with the simple magic of your spoken words. Your Apple Vision Pro awaits, ready to listen and obey!

Bonus Tip:

Train your voice recognition! Practice using a variety of accents, tones, and speaking speeds to improve the accuracy of your voice commands. The more you interact with your Vision Pro through voice, the smoother and more personalized your digital experiences will become.

Additionally, keep these aspects of Siri in mind:

Privacy matters: Be aware of when you're activating Siri in public or around sensitive information.

Accessibility options: Apple Vision Pro caters to diverse needs. Explore alternative input methods and voice control settings for an inclusive experience.

Continuous learning: Siri is constantly evolving with new features and capabilities. Stay updated to ensure you're leveraging her full potential.

Embrace the hands-free future with Siri as your guide! Let your voice become your command tool, explore the boundless possibilities of virtual and augmented reality, and discover the magic of interacting with the world around you simply by speaking your mind.

CHAPTER NINE

Safe and Responsible Use of Apple Vision Pro

Guidelines for avoiding VR sickness and discomfort

The Apple Vision Pro unlocks a universe of captivating experiences, but just like any powerful tool, its responsible use is paramount. Let's delve into essential guidelines for safe and ethical exploration of augmented and virtual reality, ensuring your journey through the digital realm is healthy, enjoyable, and enriching.

Prioritize Physical Well-being:

Mind the Clock: Take breaks every 20-30 minutes, allowing your eyes and brain to rest. Marathon VR sessions can lead to fatigue, discomfort, and potential health complications.

Move Your Body: Don't get lost in the sedentary world of VR! Stand up, stretch, and engage in physical activities regularly to counteract the prolonged stationary periods.

Listen to Your Body: Headaches, dizziness, and nausea can be warning signs of overexertion. Pay attention to your physical cues and step away from the Vision Pro if you experience any discomfort.

Protect Your Eyes:

Dim the Lights: Excessive screen time in VR can strain your eyes. Adjust the brightness settings and avoid using your Vision Pro in overly bright environments.

Focus on the Distant: Give your eyes a break from close-up focus. Look into the distance or focus on real-world objects every few minutes to prevent eye strain.

Consider Age Restrictions: Children's eyes are still developing. Follow Apple's recommendations and prioritize other forms of play for younger users.

Maintain Mental and Emotional Balance:

Step Back from Reality: Escape the real world in moderation. Excessive VR immersion can disconnect you from your surroundings and responsibilities.

Manage Expectations: Not all VR experiences are created equal. Some may contain intense situations or disturbing content. Choose experiences that align with your comfort level and emotional well-being.

Stay Grounded: Maintain healthy social interactions and physical activities outside of VR. Remember, the real world offers invaluable experiences and connections.

Beyond Yourself: Ethical Considerations:

Respect Privacy: Be mindful of filming or recording others in VR without their consent. Respect individual privacy boundaries in both the real and virtual worlds.

Avoid Distractions: Using VR in potentially dangerous situations like driving or operating machinery is irresponsible and puts yourself and others at risk.

Promote Inclusivity: Be mindful of diverse needs and limitations. Advocate for accessible VR experiences and avoid discriminatory or offensive behavior in the digital realm.

Remember, the Apple Vision Pro is a powerful tool for exploration, connection, and creativity. By prioritizing your physical and mental well-being, practicing responsible digital citizenship, and engaging in ethical virtual interactions, you can navigate the digital frontier safely and enrich your journey through augmented and virtual realities.

Bonus Tip:

Stay informed! As VR technology evolves, new guidelines and considerations may emerge. Regularly check trusted sources and research best practices to ensure your continued safe and responsible enjoyment of the Vision Pro.

Maintaining physical and mental well-being during use

Your Apple Vision Pro opens a door to exhilarating adventures and captivating experiences, but like any powerful tool, it requires mindful use to ensure your physical and mental well-being. Let's navigate the digital frontier with care, crafting a healthy and enriching journey through augmented and virtual realities.

Physically Fit for the Digital Quest:

The 20-30 Rule: Take breaks every 20-30 minutes, giving your eyes and brain a chance to recharge. Remember, even digital explorers need physical pitstops!

Rise and Shine: Combat VR's sedentary pull. Stand up, stretch, and engage in regular physical activity to keep your body primed for both virtual and real-world endeavors.

Listen to Your Body: Headaches, dizziness, or nausea are your body's signals for a timeout. Stop using the Vision Pro immediately and take a break if you experience any discomfort.

Protecting Your Precious Peepers:

Dim the Lights: Excessive screen time in VR can strain your eyes. Adjust the brightness settings and avoid using your Vision Pro in overly bright environments.

Focus on the Faraway: Give your eyes a break from close-up focus. Look into the distance or focus on real-world objects every few minutes to prevent eye strain.

Age Matters: Children's eyes are still developing. Follow Apple's recommendations and prioritize other forms of play for younger users.

Mental Equilibrium in the Digital Realm:

Escape Wisely: While VR offers a welcome respite, moderation is key. Remember, the real world deserves your attention, too. Prioritize social interactions and activities outside of VR to maintain a healthy balance.

Manage Expectations: Not all VR experiences are created equal. Choose content that aligns with your comfort level and emotional well-being. If an experience feels unsettling, don't hesitate to take a break or exit altogether.

Stay Grounded: Immerse yourself in digital worlds, but don't forget the real one. Maintain healthy social connections and physical activities outside of VR to ensure a fulfilling and **balanced life.**

Ethical Exploration: Be a Good Digital Citizen:

Respect Privacy: Filming or recording others in VR without their consent is not only rude, but can also infringe on their privacy. Remember, the golden rule applies even in the digital realm.

Distractions and Danger: Using VR in potentially dangerous situations like driving or operating machinery is irresponsible and puts yourself and others at risk. Stay alert and grounded in the real world.

Inclusivity is Key: Advocate for accessible VR experiences and be mindful of diverse needs and limitations. Treat everyone with respect and avoid discriminatory or offensive behavior in the digital space.

Remember, your Apple Vision Pro is a powerful tool for exploration, connection, and creativity. By prioritizing your physical and mental well-being, practicing responsible digital citizenship, and engaging in ethical virtual interactions, you can navigate the digital frontier with confidence, ensuring a safe, healthy, and enriching journey through augmented and virtual realities.

Bonus Tip:

Stay informed! As VR technology evolves, new guidelines and best practices may emerge. Regularly check trusted sources and research for updates to ensure your continued safe and responsible enjoyment of the Vision Pro.

Let's explore the wondrous worlds of VR together, but always with an eye towards physical and mental well-being. Your digital adventures are waiting, so grab your Vision Pro, take a deep breath, and embark on a healthy and ethical journey through the boundless possibilities of the digital realm!

CHAPTER TEN

Cleaning and Maintaining Your Apple Vision Pro

Proper cleaning techniques for the headset and controllers

Your Apple Vision Pro is a gateway to breathtaking adventures and immersive experiences, but just like any treasured tool, it requires proper care to maintain its pristine condition and optimal performance. Let's delve into the essential cleaning and maintenance techniques for your headset and controllers, ensuring your digital explorations remain crystal clear and smooth-running.

Headset Hygiene:

Gentle Giants: Softness is key! Use a microfiber cloth, preferably dampened with a 70% isopropyl alcohol solution, to wipe down the lenses and exterior surfaces. Harsh chemicals and abrasive cloth are enemies of your Vision Pro.

Sweat it Out: After an intense VR session, don't let sweat linger. Wipe down the headset with a damp microfiber cloth, focusing on the facial interface and areas that come into contact with your skin. Consider using sweat-wicking accessories for long play sessions.

Light and Breezy: Don't leave your Vision Pro in direct sunlight or extreme temperatures. Store it in a cool, dry place when not in use, ideally in its protective case to prevent dust and scratches.

Controller Cleanliness:

Wipe Away the Grime: Just like the headset, use a damp microfiber cloth to clean the controllers. Pay extra attention to the buttons, joysticks, and any crevices where dirt or grime might accumulate.

Silicone Savvy: If your controllers have removable silicone grips, take them off and wash them gently with water and mild soap. Let them air dry completely before reattaching them.

Charge Wisely: Avoid charging your controllers for extended periods when not in use. Overcharging can shorten their lifespan. Aim for regular, moderate charging cycles for optimal battery health.

Bonus Tips:

Preventative Measures: Invest in a lens cover or screen protector to keep dust and scratches at bay while your Vision Pro is tucked away.

Deep Clean Occasionally: For stubborn grime or stains, consider using a specialized VR cleaning kit with pre-moistened wipes specifically designed for delicate electronics.

Warranty & Support: Don't hesitate to contact Apple Support if you encounter any cleaning or maintenance issues beyond your comfort level. Your warranty and their expertise are there to help!

Remember, a clean and well-maintained Apple Vision Pro is your passport to uninterrupted virtual adventures and captivating augmented experiences. By following these simple cleaning and maintenance tips, you can ensure your digital journeys remain clear, comfortable, and free from technical hiccups. So, grab your microfiber cloth, embrace the gentle touch, and keep your Vision Pro sparkling for countless sessions to come!

Additional Pro Tip: Consider cleaning your Vision Pro before sharing it with others. This not only maintains hygiene but also ensures a comfortable and enjoyable experience for everyone.

Troubleshooting common issues and getting support

Even the most cutting-edge technology like your Apple Vision Pro can encounter occasional hiccups. But fear not, intrepid explorer! This guide equips you with troubleshooting tips for common issues and points you towards the right support resources to ensure your immersive adventures remain smooth and uninterrupted.

Common Glitches and Possible Solutions:

Tracking troubles:

Symptoms: Shaky image, inaccurate hand and eye tracking, objects appearing jittery.

Possible solutions: Recalibrate your Vision Pro in a well-lit environment, ensure no reflective surfaces or interfering magnetic fields are present, check for software updates.

Display woes:

Symptoms: Blurry visuals, flickering screen, blackouts.

Possible solutions: Clean the lenses with a microfiber cloth, adjust the brightness settings, ensure your Vision Pro is properly connected to the power source, check for software updates.

Audio hiccups:

Symptoms: Crackling sounds, audio cuts out completely, volume imbalance.

Possible solutions: Restart your Vision Pro, check for loose connections or damage to the earphones, pair your

Vision Pro with the source device again, check for software updates.

Connectivity headaches:

Symptoms: Difficulty connecting to your device, frequent disconnects, slow performance.

Possible solutions: Restart both your Vision Pro and your device, ensure you're within Bluetooth range, check for software updates on both devices, consider resetting your network settings.

Remember: These are just some common issues and potential solutions. For more specific or complex problems, don't hesitate to seek support!

Support Avenues at Your Fingertips:

Apple Support: Your first line of defense. Visit the Apple Support website or app, access online troubleshooting guides, chat with a support specialist, or schedule a Genius Bar appointment if needed.

Online Communities: Tap into the expertise of fellow Vision Pro users! Engage in online forums and communities to share experiences, swap troubleshooting tips, and learn from others who might have encountered similar issues.

User Manuals and Guides: Don't underestimate the power of official documentation! Refer to the Apple Vision Pro user manual and quick start guide for detailed instructions, safety information, and troubleshooting tips specific to your device.

Bonus Tip:

Stay proactive! Regularly check for software updates for your Vision Pro and connected devices. These updates often include bug fixes and performance improvements, potentially nipping potential glitches in the bud before they disrupt your enjoyment.

Remember, you're not alone on your virtual journey. With a little troubleshooting know-how and access to the right support resources, you can overcome any glitches and confidently navigate the exhilarating world of your Apple Vision Pro. So, embrace the troubleshooting spirit, seek help when needed, and continue exploring the boundless possibilities of augmented and virtual realities!**

Additional Pro Tip: Keep your charging cable and power adapter in good condition. Damaged cables can lead to charging issues and connectivity problems. Regularly inspect them for wear and tear, and replace them if necessary.

By following these tips and remaining resourceful, you can ensure your Apple Vision Pro experiences remain glitch-free and endlessly captivating. Happy exploring!

GLOSSARY OF TERMS

General Terms:

Augmented Reality (AR): Overlays digital elements onto the real world through your Vision Pro, blurring the lines between physical and virtual environments.

Virtual Reality (VR): Creates a completely immersive digital environment that replaces your view of the real world.

Head-mounted Display (HMD): The headset portion of your Vision Pro, containing the lenses and other hardware that displays the virtual or augmented world.

Controllers: Handheld devices used to interact with the digital environment in VR, often featuring buttons, joysticks, and touchpads.

Field of View (FOV): The width of the virtual or augmented world you can see through your Vision Pro.

Haptic Feedback: Vibrations and sensations in the controllers and headset that simulate touch and interaction with virtual objects.

Eye Tracking: Technology that tracks your eye movements and uses them to control the digital environment, like focusing on objects or selecting menus.

Voice Control: Using your voice to navigate and interact with the Vision Pro, like launching apps, asking questions, or issuing commands.

Siri: Your virtual assistant in the Vision Pro, available to answer questions, perform tasks, and control your digital experience.

Advanced Terms:

CAVE Automatic Virtual Environment (CAVE): A room-sized VR system that projects digital images onto walls and floor, creating a fully immersive environment for multiple users.

Mixed Reality (MR): Blends aspects of AR and VR, placing virtual objects within the real world but allowing interaction with both.

Dollhouse View: A zoomed-out view of your virtual environment, allowing you to see the bigger picture and navigate more easily.

Locomotion: Moving around within a VR environment, using techniques like teleportation, smooth locomotion, or physical walking in place.

Metaverse: A hypothetical future state of the internet where virtual and augmented reality are interwoven with the real world, creating a persistent and interconnected digital space.

Non-fungible Token (NFT): A unique digital asset stored on a blockchain, used to represent ownership of virtual items like art or collectibles.

Point-of-View (POV): The perspective from which you experience the virtual environment, usually simulated as your own eyes.

Positional Audio: Immersive sound that changes dynamically as you move your head in the VR environment, mimicking the way you hear sound in the real world.

Safety and Well-being Terms:

VR Sickness: Motion sickness symptoms like nausea and dizziness that some users experience in VR due to sensory mismatch.

20-30 Rule: Take breaks every 20-30 minutes during VR sessions to avoid eye strain and fatigue.

Physical Activities: Engage in regular physical activity outside of VR to counteract the sedentary nature of prolonged VR use.

Mental Well-being: Choose VR experiences that align with your comfort level and emotional well-being, and maintain a balance with real-world interactions.

Responsible Digital Citizenship: Respect others' privacy in VR, avoid using VR in potentially dangerous situations, and promote inclusivity in the digital realm.

Remember, this glossary is just a starting point. As VR technology evolves, new terms and concepts will emerge. Stay curious, keep exploring, and don't hesitate to ask for further clarification if you encounter unfamiliar terminology in your digital adventures!